Self-Discipline Guidebook

The best Guide to Stop Procrastination and Achieve Your Goals. Build strong Daily Habits and begin a new life. Build Mental Toughness and start Achieve Your Goals.

Written By

James Foster

© Copyright 2021 - All rights reserved.

The content contained within this book may not be reproduced, duplicated or transmitted without direct written permission from the author or the publisher.

Under no circumstances will any blame or legal responsibility be held against the publisher, or author, for any damages, reparation, or monetary loss due to the information contained within this book. Either directly or indirectly.

Legal Notice:

This book is copyright protected. This book is only for personal use. You cannot amend, distribute, sell, use, quote or paraphrase any part, or the content within this book, without the consent of the author or publisher.

Disclaimer Notice:

Please note the information contained within this document is for educational and entertainment purposes only. All effort has been executed to present accurate, up to date, and reliable, complete information. No warranties of any kind are declared or implied. Readers acknowledge that the author is not engaging in the rendering of legal, financial, medical or professional advice. The content within this book has been derived from various sources. Please consult a licensed professional before attempting any techniques outlined in this book.

By reading this document, the reader agrees that under no circumstances is the author responsible for any losses, direct or indirect, which are incurred as a result of the use of information contained within this document, including, but not limited to, — errors, omissions, or inaccuracies.

Table of Contents

INTRODUCTION 7

MEASURING YOUR MENTAL TOUGHNESS 9

MENTAL TOUGHNESS FOR BUSINESS COMPANIES AND BUSINESS TEAMS .. 17

MENTAL TOUGHNESS IN POLITICS 27

MENTAL TOUGHNESS IN MILITARY 29

RELATIONSHIP BETWEEN MENTAL TOUGHNESS AND FOCUS 39

WHAT IS FOCUS? 41

FOCUS IN BUSINESS 53

THE MAJOR VARIANCE 81

CONCLUSION 103

INTRODUCTION

Thank you for purchasing this book!

You have ever wondered, what makes somebody a good athlete? Or some good leader? Or a right relative? Why do some people achieve their goals while others fail?

What would make the difference?

We usually respond to those questions by thinking about top performers' talent. He must be the lab's most ingenious scientist. She's faster on the ground than anybody else. He is a brilliant strategist on the market.

But I think we all know that the story has more to offer than that.

When you begin to look into it, your talent and intelligence don't play as big a part as you might think. The research studies I found tell you that knowledge accounts for only 30 percent of your achievement and, that's on the upper hand.

What makes the effect higher than talent or intelligence? Mental tenacity.

Research is starting to show that your mental resilience — or "grit," as it is called — plays a more critical role in achieving your fitness, business, and life goals than anything else. That is good news because you can't do much about the genes from which you have been born, but you can do much to develop mental toughness.

Enjoy your reading!

MEASURING YOUR MENTAL TOUGHNESS

Measuring your mental toughness is just one source of information. It's essential to recognize that there will be other types of evidence about your mental toughness, such as how well under pressure you do.

Through answering the following statements, take stock of your degree of mental toughness. Answer each with seldom, sometimes, or always.

- When unforeseen workplace events occur, they derail me._____.

- I'm dependable. _____

- When I'm under pressure, I throw in the towel. _____

- I will relate to the challenges that lie before me._____.

- At the first hint of trouble, I walk away. _____

- I still think about making the same mistake I made recently._____.

- When under pressure, I keep rereading the same details. _____

Check your reactions. They are a snapshot in time. Remember, mental toughness is a characteristic that determines how you will perform a task and how effectively you will respond to your environment in some respects. It is a key factor to perform to the best of your capabilities and can be developed or strengthened in many ways.

How do you know you are mentally tough?

If you are cultivating mental toughness, what evidence should you look for that tells you? How do you know you are psychologically tough? Here's a list of partial corroborations. Maybe you can find a few more.

Instead of losing your cool, you remain calm and focused under pressure.

You make a commitment, and instead of breaking it, you follow through.

Instead of rigidly fighting them, you adjust to the obstacles that come before you.

At the first hint of uncertainty, you have a stick-to-activity, instead of giving up.

Instead of naysayers, you surround yourself with more positive people and with negative attitudes.

When you agree to be mentally more energetic, the outlook for achievement and fulfillment of more is brighter, wealthier, and more fulfilled. You are starting to develop into a more credible and trustworthy human being. Make your creation gentle and cautious as you navigate the often confusing, often treacherous waters of business, relationships, and life. Taking on this type of personal and professional development is like training a new gym muscle; it takes time, commitment, and dedication, and it doesn't happen overnight!

Remember the adage "Rome wasn't made in a day." And for a more positive saying, always remember this resilient phrase "NEVER GIVE UP" while confronting a situation that may be daunting, confrontational, or overwhelming. Oh, please come on! From your roots, you have come a long way to give up.

MENTAL TOUGHNESS ACTION TECHNIQUES

Pay close attention to your feelings. Turn from worrying about cruise control to being conscious of what you are doing.

Monitor your reaction to all situations, emotionally. At the very first sign or feeling of pressure or not wanting to stand up to a challenge, stop what you're doing right away, take a few deep breaths and be both in mind and action. Then ask yourself, "Do I allow certain events or circumstances to control how I react emotionally, or do I control how I want to respond?" Visualize yourself as powerful, resourceful, and victorious when faced with difficult situations. This technique can be used to improve a sales pitch or a sport's accuracy.

Two realistic ways to develop the mental toughness that you need in business and life:

If I had to choose only one attribute and feature that I was able to take away from high school that had a significant impact on my life, it would be mental toughness, without a doubt. My teachers loved me throughout my secondary school and engaged me in so many extracurricular activities such as debates, Quiz, Fellowships executives, School prefects, Competitions, etc. I used to be under severe pressure because I had too much involved in it, and at one point, I felt like they were purposely punishing me. And my colleagues ask how I got to be brilliant because I've always been stressed out. I'll be grateful to them forever because of all those intense feelings, stresses, and emotions that support my life today. I have to warn you that going on stage or pedestals and facing the audience is not an easy one. The fear that comes with it is mysterious, and the rate that your heart beats at. There are moments when you will forget all of the things you know in the presence of fear that you will face the crowd. The terror that comes with it is mysterious, and the pace that your heart beats at. There are times when you will forget all of the things you know in the wake of fear that you will face the crowd.

Of course, I learned the immense importance of teamwork, community, leadership, and other vital values, but what I am most grateful for is the strength that was instilled in me from my high school. I talk with faith wherever I go today, even when I am incorrect, but I always stand to be corrected. But first, you'll need to listen to my own opinion and then prove me wrong. I am ever known for my confidence and composure.

If you believe that football players or other professional athletes are raised with a different kind of mental toughness and that it is second nature for them right away, you are mistaken. Mental toughness is something that you can improve and develop over time regardless of what you do for a living.

If you feel mentally defeated, the chances are small that you will ever get to where you want to go. Whether we are thinking about sports or industry, winning, first and foremost, will be absolutely necessary. When you have a phenomenally positive mentality, there is nothing that you can't or become.

A big part of having a centered attitude is being able to keep moving forward when the going gets extremely hard, staying positive when disappointment threatens and persisting over and over until you eventually reach your destination. That's the true definition of mental toughness: showing a tremendous amount of confidence, battling, and commitment toward a mission you're pursuing with a passion. When you look at any group of high performers regardless of industry, you will quickly realize that they have shown the exceptional mental toughness to get where they are.

One of the best ways to build mental toughness is through the daily practice of being conscious. Mindfulness is all about focusing your energies and emotions without any judgment on the present moment. When I was in high school, I was initially introduced to the influence of mindfulness training. I was about to go to the stage for a discussion, and the crowd had overcome me, and the spirit of fear had already come into me. My instructor in the class spoke to me about how to conquer the moment and control it.

Not long ago, I had an opportunity to run the company for my mother. It was more or less like I was working as a contractor here and there to make the companies. For me, it was the right moment because I always love to see the money flowing in.

I can give two practical ways, based on my own experiences, which can help you build mental toughness and resilience in business, starting today.

1.   Practice continual watchfulness.

It's a game-changer to practice mindfulness every day. Studies not only show the importance of being conscious and describing the amazing benefits it offers, but people like me are recommending it based on personal experience.

Mindfulness calms the mind down from the noisy and chaotic world in which we live, and that calmness, in effect, equips you with the energy and peace of mind to continue moving forward even in the face of extreme difficulty. Being in sync with the present moment and living entirely right where you are at present helps to diminish the anxiety that holds back other people and gives them the strength to concentrate on what is most important.

Practicing everyday mindfulness doesn't just help you build mental toughness; it can change your life in so many different ways, such as reducing your daily anxiety and dramatically improving your overall wellbeing.

2.   Come out of your usual comfort zone.

This one may be much tougher than practicing conscientiousness, but making it a daily habit to venture out of your comfort zone creates incredible strength. Just as you would go to the gym to make your muscles grow stronger physically, getting out of your comfort zone every day is what allows you to improve your mental toughness capability.

While I had the opportunity to be the manager of my mother, she'd send me to places she cannot send her employees, more complicated tasks. I could be gone all day, at times trying to make it happen. I'd come back home and crumble as Tyson Fury had thoroughly beaten me. And any day I feel reluctant when she sends me on those kinds of errands, she would remind me who I'm going to be saying, "The days you feel most uncomfortable are the days you get to know yourself better and how amazing you can be."

The more I try to step out of my comfort zone, the stronger and better I feel, no matter how uncomfortable it may be at the moment. One of the first things that I do when I schedule my day the night before is to ask myself how I can venture out of my comfort zone for that particular day. By always playing it safe and working only out of the limits of your comfort zone, you cannot develop mental toughness and become resilient.

In short, if you want to step into your grandeur and become the best version of yourself, being healthy and mentally tough is non-negotiable. Give the two practices a try. They might well be helping you get there.

MENTAL TOUGHNESS FOR BUSINESS COMPANIES AND BUSINESS TEAMS

We all agree that 80 percent of success is psychological, and 20 percent of success is ability. We all need it all. You've got financial targets to meet by quarter-end. And it is not your team that is involved. You want the leadership team to be as focused on everyone. But it is not. You meet with the management team to explore morale-enhancing strategies and improve employee engagement.

- A team-building, morale raising program

- A core values awareness plan

- Feeding low-performing workers and hiring new talent

But the fact is, these are band-aid remedies that give mixed results and are seldom permanent solutions.

The number-one cause of an employee's low performance is disappointment in situations that they feel helpless to change. It could result from one of these issues or a combination of:

- Coworker relationships

- Market conditions

- Workplace climate

- Corporate culture

- Product offerings

- Manager relationships

- Missing position

Here is the commonality when an employee experiences a hurdle they feel powerless to resolve, either:

- Protest against it

- Put it up

- Ignore it

This results in frustration and a weakening desire to succeed.

What's missing is Mindset and communication strategies at a high level. Those two elements regain the employee's autonomy and provide them with a path to success regardless of the difficulty.

This is what success in mental toughness offers.

Sport psychologists often use the word "mental toughness" to describe: "a built psychological edge that helps athletes cope with their sport's demands, stresses, and distractions."

When an athlete faces a fear or repetitive behavior pattern that interferes with their success at their highest capacity, mental toughness preparation is what helps them to overcome their reactive inclinations, stay focused, calm, and in control at all times.

In the business context, it is the same. Mental toughness preparation provides access to on-demand problem-solving skills for business executives and their teams. This enables them to transcend situational and interpersonal organizational obstacles rapidly so that they can work with order, dedication, ease, and productivity to achieve common goals.

Much critical business value of mental toughness can be difficult. The overwhelming majority of successful professionals would agree it is not easy to do their job. The crucial differentiator between consistently successful professionals and those who fall short is the desire to persevere when difficult times occur. Specific values of corporate mental toughness include:

1. It allows you to overcome your fear— one of the most important steps on the path to mental toughness is to overcome the fear of failure. While this does not mean a complete lack of anxiety, a mentally tough individual knows that there is nothing to gain from stress or worry. It is essential to take time to consider tactics, but once a decision is made, a mentally tough person can follow the goal aggressively, committing himself to the task while putting aside fear.

2. It lets you set goals & compete with yourself— climbing to the top with mental toughness. In times of adversity, aggressive goals can carry a person. By fixing on the outcome of their efforts, obstacles, or temporary setbacks don't easily dissuade a mentally tough professional. There is a clear correlation between mentally tough people and those who are competitive, and the most moving, satisfying, and safe kind of competition can be challenging oneself. An individual

can genuinely develop only by being challenged to exceed expectations, and that includes professional skills.

3. It allows you to accept criticism and then kill it — Criticism should be recognized and valued, especially if it comes from those whose opinion the professional trusts hold. They help you through the toughening process. A professional can greatly boost their professional development by humbling himself and listening to feedback. Still, it takes a lot of mental fortitude to accept constructive criticism and use it to make improvements. A genuinely resilient business brain knows that even the harshest feedback from the staunchest opponent can provide valuable insight into vulnerabilities that can then be converted into strengths.

4. It gingers you into practicing serenity and living in the present— Remaining focused is one of the most important aspects of a mentally tough business professional. Comprehending the Serenity Prayer's overarching message and being ever aware of the current situation would help a professional to reflect and work more effectively. In short, viewing past mistakes as learning opportunities, and distinguishing between circumstances that are and are not in the control of a professional, would allow the detachment of personal emotions, preventing a negative effect on self-effectiveness. Successful professionals keep

things in perspective and channel their energies towards the outcomes which are within the control locus of the person.

5.   It helps you in the Don't Give in or Give up situations— being an entrepreneur, there are times you are going to doubt yourself. Yes! You are reading it right. The world is not all about sunshine and rainbow, but it is a very mean and nasty place. I don't care about how tough you are; it will beat you to your knees and keep you there permanently if you let it. The tough times have not come to stay, but rather have they come to pass. So many successful entrepreneurs and professionals share stories of incredibly tough times, self-doubt, and the desire to throw in the towel. They found a way, however, for you to hear the story, and persevered through the adversity. Simply put, never give in, compromise your passion, or give up on an objective. Do not cool to any light. The most characteristic feature of all successful entrepreneurs and professionals is the ability to keep going when others have given up, and that takes a lot of determination and mental toughness.

6.   It encourages you to work hard and don't moan and inspires you - Whining and lamentation have no place in business. Such COMMENTS ARE A WASTE OF TIME for the person and all those around them if comments are not made in an effort to fix an issue or change a situation. Instead of focusing

attention on the negative aspects of a situation, a mentally tough person would dedicate himself to hard work, finding a way, and achieving the goal.

Sheer grit and determination will help make great things happen to a professional. A person with mental toughness naturally tries to work out their competition, as they know that hard work can lead to consistent success, and very often does.

10 Mental toughness Fundamentals for Entrepreneurs

Mental toughness in sports is defined as the ability to focus on and implement solutions, particularly in the face of adversity. If anyone ever wanted mental toughness in industry, he's an entrepreneur. Investors tell me that startup success is all about execution when confronting aggressive rivals and overcoming the resistance to change from customers.

1. Define the win for your business: It's not a parlor game for a startup. It's all about solving a problem with a for-profit startup that embodies real pain, with real customers who are willing and able to pay for a solution. That is all about making the world a better place for social entrepreneurs. Find what it takes to win early, or you'll lose by default.

2. Adopt a business vision that suits your self-image: You need a long-term vision that promotes self-realization and self-image as well as business success in every situation. Evaluate your strengths and weaknesses and see how they will

lead to business success. If your enthusiasm is not fueled by the dream and your skills suit, you won't like the lifestyle.

3. Establish real business strategies and processes: Things that have not been established are difficult to achieve, and the steps to get there are not visible. I propose a one-year business focus, with a maximum of three product priorities and three process targets.

4. Prioritize the preferences: The motto of every entrepreneur should be prioritized or perish. Accountability includes the breaking and organizing of your big product targets into regular process goals. Don't become distracted by the unimportant.

5. Practice accountability by self-assessment: learn every day to look in the mirror. No assessment means no understanding of how you are doing, and that does not give you any reason for the change. Excellent performance requires no perfection, which is impossible to achieve.

6. Control your emotions to control your performance: learn how to control the level of arousal and alertness of your nerves and emotions. Through ensuring basic mental health and physical fitness and by mentally educating yourself, you will work more effectively, and the successes will increase.

7.   Prepare to say the right thing: Respond to the three most common situations that you face. Develop and record templates, such as your elevator pitch, to help you and your team keep attention for key interactions. They build trust and lower the anxiety that often interferes with leadership success.

8.   Every day prepare your mind mentally: You should improve your mind every day, just like a muscle. Every day complete a mental workout to significantly improve your concentration and regularly execute the performance. It's one of the most effective methods known to train your mind and body to remain under control and perform to your capacity.

9.   Create a persistent and positive outlook on the solution: One of the most critical pieces of your mental toughness puzzle is replacing all negative thinking. Approach all solutions; one step at a time, where any change to the present situation is one step. Know a focus on issues alone is likely to cause further problems.

10.   Find a way to get it done when you set your mind to do something, no matter what: While the mental stage is a constant concentration on the solution, determination is the level of action that makes solutions materialize. Discipline delivers performance in this way. Make discipline a habit by minimizing the opportunity and practicing consciously.

To succeed and lead in today's business environment, we all need these basics of mental toughness. This requires more than just market knowledge and technical know-how. That's the fun part of the most intense entrepreneurs' challenge. If it was easy, it could happen to anyone. Are you set to step up to the plate?

MENTAL TOUGHNESS IN POLITICS

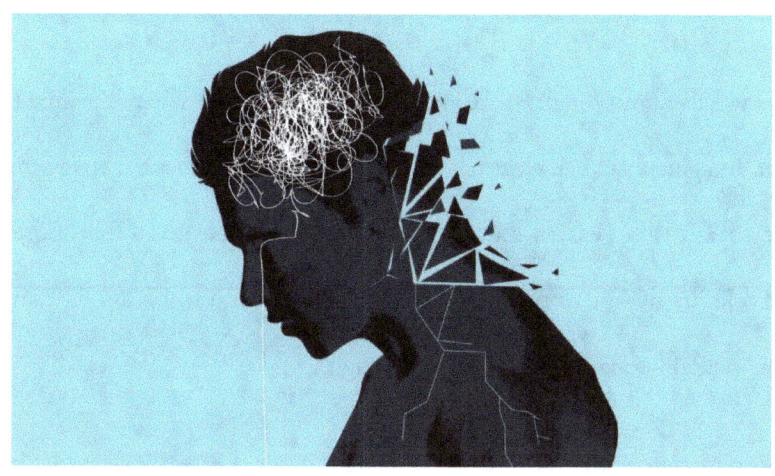

One of the influental mentally tough people in the world is the politicians. In politics, you win and lose. Being a politician can make you restless because you are serving the people; only if you are not selfish enough to help yourself. Politicians do not get involved in menial tasks or works, but you wonder why they get tired quickly. Okay, let me put it this way. Why do you get tired after writing an examination? This same reason applies to politicians.

Thinking makes you get tired irrespective of how strong and tough you are. Politicians are one of the most thinking people in the world.

Apart from that, the stress that comes with an aspiration of posts and campaigns is immeasurable; trying to convince people and thinking of different strategies of winning their hearts. It is difficult to win a girl's heart, not to talk of the heart of the masses. You must be extraordinary and a profound thinker.

Now let us talk about the pressure and how tensed they get when it is time for an election. Imagine losing an election, how will they feel and in what state of health will they be? It is not easy. I must say that politics is a tense and full of pressure affair. So let us try and appreciate these people. For you to be a politician, you must be mentally tough. Even Jesus was tough.

I could remember when I was aspiring to be the General Secretary in my department. A lot happened, and my colleagues told me to give up that I cannot win the election. Being a mentally tough man, I did not give up, even when everyone was not supporting me. I went on and did my campaigns alone most times. I was mocked but continued. My quality spoke for me while I was meeting with people one on one, including my opponents, and I started gaining an audience. All my opponents stepped down, and I won the election unopposed. You must be mentally tough, I repeat, you must be mentally tough. Mental toughness could earn you what you do not deserve.

MENTAL TOUGHNESS IN MILITARY

Mental toughness is, as inferred, a state of mind. An average person can learn this without being part of the military. Mental toughness is endurance, the willingness to stick to something regardless of challenges, to be objective-oriented, always to try to improve, to be reliable and consistent. I believe that mental toughness is being fueled either by a commitment to oneself or by a dedication to a greater cause. Ideally, both are.

By setting goals, pushing oneself a little harder, and working for small victories, any human can develop mental toughness. Mentally tough people are always willing to (metaphorically) climb up the mountain in the rain because they know the reward is at the top of the mountain.

Mentally hard people know what's right for themselves, their future, and they're willing to show restraint, courage, and sacrifice to attain their goals. That's why we often see the most successful people not being the ones with natural talent, but those who had to overcome obstacles through hard work, determination, and commitment to achieving their goals.

The military does a great job of drawing on an individual's inspiration and personal goals. If you want to be a parachutist, a Ranger, a SEAL, or a Green Beret, you need to volunteer, practice, prepare yourself, and prove mentally strong. At Ranger School, the students are piled up with little sleep, long walks, limited food, and leadership stress to see if they will stand up to the pressure or leave. Training for SEAL and Special Forces offers similar challenges in seeing who will quit and who has "grit" mentally stable People do not leave.

Often, the military taps into the other catalyst or mental toughness motivator, which is a higher cause. Those who join the army have a love of institutions, way of life, flag, constitution, and values that make this nation great. They are trained to fight for those ideals to continue to exist. They are trained to fight for those ideals to continue to exist. A profound devotion and willingness to sacrifice is etched upon their hearts for the cause and the soldiers they are fighting alongside.

Being mentally hard requires that you continue to compete when your mind needs you to stop. Human beings have a "safety switch" in our brain that asks us to stop so we don't get hurt. Soldiers are survivors born naturally designed to conserve energy, store food, and simply live to survive another day. There are moments when you really should turn off that part of your brain. You realize when you do this, which your body is ten times stronger than your brain will let it be. Training programs in the field of special operations help them tap into this mentality. Still, often your life experiences and practices will create resilience and mental toughness that no one can overcome.

Here is a top ten list of common denominators in many people who have accomplished great things in their lives and are still moving towards more substantial and more extensive objectives:

1. Regular Focus / Persistence–Never Start! Do what you need to do every day and when you're tired, feeling lazy, and so on. It doesn't matter whether it's physical fitness, preparing for an exam, working on a deadline, or just getting out of bed with a positive attitude every day-do it no matter what. You might find that all you needed was a good meal and hydration to give you the energy needed to stay focused and finish or begin a new task.

No-one gets tough psychologically overnight. It lasts for a lifetime. Some of the toughest people in life know they have some degree of resilience, but they still tell every day they have to work on it.

2.Stay Motivated: Why are you putting yourself through exhausting preparation, working long hours, or studying? This question has to be answered—not me. Motivating you is not the job of anybody; it's all SELF-MOTIVATION that keeps you ongoing. Have goals that you see each day come closer and closer to fruition one step at a time. Prepare mentally for the weeks, months, or even years required to reach where one day you want to be.

3.Have a quote resonating with you—There are plenty of fantastic motivational quotes to get you going and keep you moving. One for me, in particular, is, "I don't have to trick people who believe in me." Find one for you which fits. Find a poster or do a poster and see it every day. Say it when the need arises.

4.Train to Compete—Not Just Survive: In terms of special ops training programs, athletic events, or even business—this is the biggest difference between those who graduate or excel and those who don't. You should aim to be in the type of shape and attitude that, in many cases, at least some will allow you to win or be in the top 10 percent of the class. In general, too many of us just get "putting in their time" by every day and barely live. Knowing you're trapped in survival mode is a recognition that can be the first step in learning how to change your life and succeed in your life for the first time.

5.   Dissociation Training: There is a fine line between mental toughness and insanity, but there's no dumb technique if it keeps you alive when it's a life-or-death situation. Essentially, you can play with how much pain, discomfort, and even fear? That is an immensely successful item. Dissociation means being able to handle teachers yelling at you, cold water freezing you, sand strangling you, and fatigue slowing you down and not letting it get into your brain. In these dissociation skills, there's a bit of "find your happy place," but you still have to focus on the mission at hand and not just be some zombie who can't follow orders stuck in some state. You can practice this skill with mundane, monotonous, long workouts such as long runs, boxing, swimming, high repetition pyramid PTs that can get pretty boring if you don't have the ability to think of anything else aside from counting reps, miles and time.

6.   Laugh: One of the best ways to get through the daily grind is to find humor in what happens to you each day. Find humor in what challenges you are facing. When you go through a stressful event, you'd be shocked how a funny remark or action can lighten the mood and keep you focused on the task at hand. Having fun and laughing in a group setting will bind a team like no other. You

have to laugh by yourself, as it will help change your attitude, compose yourself, and overcome any negative thoughts you may have at the moment.

7.   Know Your Weakness–Make it a Strength: You must have a degree of inner knowledge and know that there will be things you simply are not good at. I find that I have to check-in and use a certain level of mental toughness to keep going while focusing on my weaknesses than if working on something I was naturally good at doing. Be true to yourself.

8.   Plan your dive-Dive your plan: soldiers are taught how to "Dirt Dive" during training. This is a clear walk-through of a mission where each process of the task is performed step by step, explaining how to achieve the desired outcome. Discussing and creating contingency plans is one of the results which help to be flexible immediately in case something goes wrong. Build various routes to accomplish your goal. There may be 3–4 different ways of getting from A to B. Consider any choice and don't get discouraged if your original plan fails. Switch to plan B or even plan C. Stay focused on goals to the end.

9.   Big goals with sub-goals: parallel this can also be achieved in the business world by keeping track of weekly, monthly, quarterly goals, and the next thing you know about your annual projections, even if you need to change course to get there. But if you don't appraise, you won't know how to change direction.

10.   Stay Positive: Planning and positive thinking go a long way. If it's not in the schedule or strategy, it doesn't happen, so make sure that your plans and actions stay positive. Now and then, you'll have negative thoughts and questions that pop into your mind. A trick to avoid being overwhelmingly negative is called "Mark it and Tame it." The next time a negative thought or doubt appears in your mind or is spoken to your team by another, give it a stupid name like "rubbish." Then say it out loud, so you say it and hear it, "I can't think of" rubbish "anymore." This may take a few practice rounds, but it works to help you stay positive. Naming a thought takes away the strength and tells you that your worries and anxieties are in control. That is solid.

I hope if you are in the military that works for you. Mental toughness tips and qualities are by no means limited to this top-ten list. There are endless ways to build your mental toughness and endurance that will help you stay empowered, think positively, and deal with stress or hardship for the rest of your life.

Hang in... And never give up.

<u>Few common tips to be a mentally strong soldier</u>

•   Breathe slowly, breathe deeply, and clear your mind: running, hiking, or climbing is one of the most challenging tasks in the military to do well, and then trying to fire a rifle or pistol accurately. It's not unusual to run 100 yards to the firing line during training, plan your weapon and then fire at a target right away. Clearly, a lifting chest and wobbly arms don't make a precise shot. Snipers are instructed to pause their breathing, lie on their back, take some deep breaths, and then clear their minds to concentrate on the single task at hand: accurately shooting. In the professional world, this technique was also of excellent service.

Before talking to an angry customer on the phone, presenting at a conference, or pitching a new customer, try: (1) Pause, (2) Focus and slow your breathing, (3) Take a few slow deep breaths, (4) clear your mind, and (5) Focus 100% on the task at hand.

This process takes just a couple of seconds but gives you exceptional power to tackle a complex task with a clear mind.

- Slow, step-by-step mental rehearsals create mastery: We all know the importance of sports, dance, gymnastics, theater, and public speaking practice and rehearsals. Military soldiers rehearse almost everything— shooting, parachuting, speaking foreign languages, assembling radios— because they know they'll encounter situations when time, resources, and security don't allow full, complete, and resource-intensive rehearsals. This is where mental rehearsals can be instrumental, the method in which you accurately visualize what the absolute perfect fulfillment of your mission looks like. This degree of thorough imagery, rehearsed continuously in your mind, is indispensable to master complex tasks using mental discipline.

- Do the best you can for the next five minutes: block the hours ahead, concentrate on doing the best you can for the next five minutes. When those five minutes pass, concentrate on doing well in the next five minutes, etc. Master your fatigue by focusing only on short periods, and finish the climb. Next time you are facing a seemingly impossible mission, try to concentrate on doing the best you can for the next five minutes and then repeat until you cross the line.

- Look and look relaxed— even if you don't feel it: One of the best ways to manage your own tension is to make sure you project an image of personal peace, serenity, and comfort, even when you're in a really difficult situation. The mere act of looking relaxed, confident, and in control of the situation actually helps you control your stress level. This aptitude helps to look confident.

RELATIONSHIP BETWEEN MENTAL TOUGHNESS AND FOCUS

I consider mental toughness as the ability to reason, think. It is the ability to control unexpected situations entirely. Being mentally tough is good, but I think we should acknowledge that it involves a process to get the desired result.

Self-discipline is the action taken as a result of everything you have thought about. Self-discipline is the ability to do what you have deeply thought about and stay consistent. While doing it, you might not even get the desired result. Why do some students go to school and still fail, despite not missing a class in a calendar year? Mental toughness helps you to make your mind that "I want to go to school." Self-discipline speaks about your attendance in school. You can't be punctual in school if you are not self-disciplined. Take it or not leave it; it is not easy to wake up very early in the morning and start preparing to go to school. There are times you will feel so bad or even sick, but you will still get up and prepare and go to school. That is self-discipline. The reason why students fail in school despite being mentally tough that against all the odds, they still want to go to school, and deploying their self-disciplines into it is simply that they fail to focus. If you fail to focus, then you will eventually get lost, and the purpose is not there any longer. So here is my summary below.

- Mental toughness- decision to go to school,

- Self-discipline- attendance in school,

- Focus- attentiveness in school.

If you are not attentive in class, you will not understand what you are being taught. If you don't know what you are being taught, then the purpose is gone. I repeat the purpose is gone.

Now let us discuss extensively about Focus.

WHAT IS FOCUS?

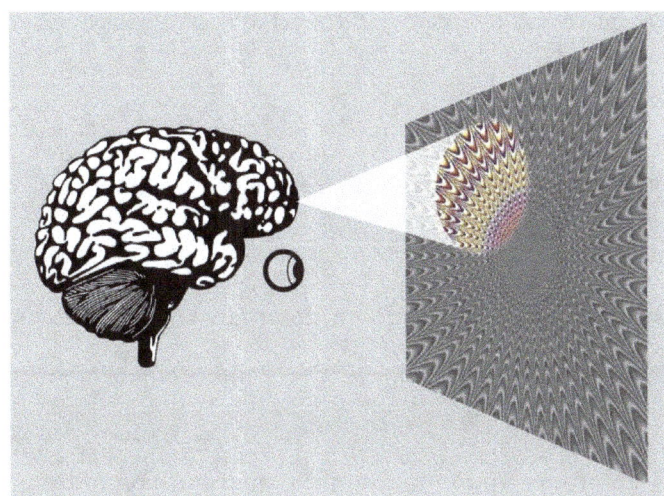

Focus is a grammatical category, according to Linguistics, which decides which part of the sentence contributes new, non-derivable, or contrastive content. The emphasis is in relation to the structure of knowledge.

Focus is, according to Mathematics, a fixed point or one of a pair of fixed points used to create a curve like an ellipse, parabola, or hyperbola.

A focus also called an image point, is the point where light rays from a spot on the object converge, according to Physics Optics. While the focus is conceptually a point, the focus is physically spatial, called the blur circle. Such non-ideal focusing can be attributed to camera optics aberrations. The smallest possible blur circle in the absence of significant aberrations is the Airy disk, which is induced by diffraction from the aperture of the optical system. Aberrations continue to get worse as the aperture diameter increases, while for wide apertures, the Airy circle is the smallest.

When light from object points converges in the picture almost as much as possible, and out of focus when light is not well converged, an image, or image point or area, is in focus. Sometimes the boundary between these is established using a "confusion circle" criterion.

To explain, in my own view, focus means paying attention or concentrating on something in particular.

When I started pushups, I used to stop when I start feeling the pain. Once I start to feel pain, I would stop. There is nothing you can tell me. Until that faithful day, when my sports adviser told me, "The real pushups start when you start to feel the pain. If you don't feel and take the pain, you are only wasting your time". Since that day, I began to focus on the moments when the pains are experienced. I had that mental toughness to make up my mind that I wanted to be doing pushups in the morning, and I was self-disciplined enough to be doing it every morning when I wake up. But where was the focus before my sports adviser spoke to me? Focusing on the wrong thing will definitely not give you the desired result. This is the reason why some students who really love to go to school don't make an excellent result.

It is important to know that you might be tough in your head and not show physically. How does it manifest and display your physical appearance? This is why I said it involves a process in which Focus is a key role player.

HOW TO USE FOCUS TO BE MENTALLY TOUGH

Mental toughness is a way of thinking that gives you the stamina and motivation to be more effective, more optimistic, and less depressed than those that don't. By modifying your behaviors and taking a more disciplined and less emotional approach to your work and life, it can be measured and created. This consists of four essential scales or characteristics, backed by a basic but scientific research survey:

- Control

- Commitment

- Challenge

- Confidence

Each one has two sub-scales or characteristics, and each has an essential part to play within the overall system.

By looking at all of these characteristics, we can easily point to Commitment as being the nearest to concentrate. I'm going to elaborate more on involvement here.

COMMITMENT

Being always focused on achieving your goals and goals, I see Commitment as the' making it happen' C because it involves your commitment and determination to set your goals and goals, your concentration on reaching them, and the action needed to achieve them without disrupting or sacrificing them.

If you are incredibly committed to this degree then faced with demanding and unyielding deadlines, you are more likely to tackle and achieve tasks and situations effortlessly. With high levels of internal resources, you are usually robust and tenacious and will definitely do whatever you need to do to achieve your goal. This latter quality makes you incredibly trustworthy because it is so crucial for you to achieve your goals.

It is necessary to find a balance, though, because too much effort and absolute emphasis on the result means that you can easily bruise people who are less dedicated along the way.

In a crisis, this is generally acceptable and indeed attractive, but far less so in the business as usual style' where you will quickly gain a reputation for being challenging and unpleasant to deal with.

If you are low on Commitment, you are likely to be easily distracted or frustrated at the other end of the scale and find it challenging to complete tasks in the face of adverse circumstances. You'll probably find it difficult to take on additional responsibilities because you're struggling and giving up too quickly when under strain.

Within the Commitment scale are two subscales:

1. GOAL ORIENTATION

As it implies, target orientation tests how driven you are by expectations and objectives, and you like to know what is expected of you when you are high. Perhaps you can envision success and imagine what will be a successful result.

Nonetheless, one of the drawbacks of being too centered is that you may often lose sight of essential non-results-focused considerations such as how your colleagues feel. You may be more about the trip than about the destination, which will frustrate you and will definitely frustrate your reaction.

A balance may be ideal depending on the position or circumstances, but in a modern working environment, being low on target orientation will almost always be detrimental. Often you will feel intimidated by the deadlines that could bring about working towards goals, and particularly the implications of not meeting them.

2. ACHIEVEMENT ORIENTATION

Achievement Orientation is the other half of the dedication equation when it comes to deciding how you can concentrate and do what it takes to achieve the objective. If you're high in this field, you're usually going to work hard, don't get distracted easily, and feel great satisfaction.

Sometimes the problem for those too high on Achievement Orientation is that they are so focused on achieving their goals that they can be inflexible and potentially miss targets that shift.

At the other end of the spectrum being low on Accomplishment Orientation, it can be challenging for individuals who are likely to give up on projects and activities more quickly than most–particularly when there are daily failures or relatively high-pressure levels.

They may find it difficult to sustain attention and mental control for more than a short period, which is becoming increasingly common in an age in which technology distracts the focus so easily.

So, how do you develop your sense of commitment?

It's important to have a sense of purpose in your life and realize what you believe in and want your legacy to be. From this, you can build a set of goals that will enable you to fulfill your objective once you achieve them. These will be regular goals in their most granular form, which you can achieve through being disciplined and concentrated. There are techniques that you can use to improve your concentration and prevent your plans from being disrupted by internal mental challenges and external distractions such as social media.

IMPORTANCE OF FOCUS IN YOUR LIFE

You are living in a fast-paced world where every day you can easily get distracted by a lot of things. You can do everything, but it's pretty impossible to become successful if you lack direction in your life. Let me clarify why concentration is important in your life and help you know why.

Focus can really change it all.

As it says-" Power flows where attention is paid to it. As you focus on something, it's getting bigger.

It's essential to understand why concentration is so important so that you can use it for your benefit.

Here are the reasons why Focus is important in your life.

1.   It helps you change your life

The focus will drastically change the way you live. If you focus on making your life better, it will slowly start to get better.

As it says, "The essence of changing is to concentrate all your attention not on the old, but on the new."

When you decide to change it, life changes, you have to get started working on shift. The more forever you concentrate, the better your life will be.

2.   This opens up more opportunities for you.

The focus will help you figure out the direction you don't even know exists. With our problems in life, we become so blind that we fail to reflect on the possibilities.

As it is said-" IF YOU FOCUS ON PROBLEMS, YOU WILL HAVE MORE PROBLEMS. WHEN YOU FOCUS ON POSSIBILITIES, WILL HAVE MORE OPPORTUNITIES.

So, in your life, you need to start looking for possibilities and open new doors to new opportunities.

Don't listen to others. Only note that in your life, concentration is important to accept the potential that is around you.

3. Focus expands your knowledge.

The focus will help you expand your knowledge and intelligence. When you start focusing on learning, awareness gradually grows.

Concentrate on learning new things every day and making lifelong learning a priority. There will be some distractions around you, though, but you need to concentrate anyway.

Focusing on increasing your awareness immediately expands your life.

4. It aids you in becoming productive at work.

Distraction is always scratching at your window. How you choose between attention and diversion, it's your decision. The focus will help you make your job more successful. It will help you focus your attention on a specific task as your primary goal. All the rest is secondary.

Reflect on being productive, but most people never concentrate on being successful. Then they focus on being occupied.

Concentration is important in your life so you can become highly productive at work and effectively do the job.

5. It helps you make your goals come true.

Your emphasis will determine the level of achievements you achieve in life. You'll hit your goals when you put your attention to accomplish something in life. Otherwise, you'll end up wasting your energy and time on useless things.

Life is like a camera; it focuses on and captures what is necessary. If you want to reach your goals, place your attention on the targets, and continue to work until you achieve them.

6. Focus allows you quicker to become successful.

No one can deter you when you're concentrated on attaining success. Successful people focus on the mission. Every single day they work for their goals. It makes them gain success quicker than anyone else.

Some people do try something, though, but never stay consistent. It becomes a barrier to their highways.

Focus is necessary to attain success in your life.

Successful individuals never allow obstacles to get in their way.

In conclusion, Focus does not get the respect that it deserves in the world, but if used correctly, it can change your life. Successful people know the importance of lifetime concentration. Your focus will decide how good you are. This will produce great results when your attention is matched with your acts.

Here are things to remember:

- Changing your life helps.

- This provides you more chances.

- Focus expands the awareness you have.

- This helps make you work more efficiently.

- This enables you to make your goals come true.

Focus allows you quicker to become effective. That's why focus in your life is vital for getting what you want in life.

FOCUS IN BUSINESS

As small business owners, it can be incredibly easy to get cases of attention deficit disorder where the next apparently good business idea catches our attention, and we leap at it like a bug flying towards a light bulb. The old saying that you seem to be accurate when you try to do too many things at once, you end up doing a whole lot of things poorly.

Great companies are created, founded, and developed by entrepreneurs who focus their day-to-day efforts on that sector. It's not by accident that people who literally live inside them build good companies, at least before they expand to the point of viability and prosperity where they could afford to bring in additional staff and leadership. Enterprise success involves focusing on the broadest definition of the word.

Steve Jobs, the founder of Apple, was known for his intense focus. He would describe what he regarded as obstacles to his mission and primary tasks, and filter out all else. If what somebody asked him wasn't a priority for that day, he just wouldn't be answering the email or even direct questions and would be doing business. His relentless enthusiasm, determination, and desire to create something else rubbed many people in the wrong direction, creating enemies for Jobs and the company, but his intensity was never diminished, and his dream of what Apple could never fail.

When Jobs returned to his company in 1997, one of his first goals was to focus an increasingly complex and diverse product line on one that could be reliably and profitably generated. He narrowed Apple's wide range of products into four packages for two different customer groups-business and consumer, which importantly saved the company. Business focus also has to do with what your company stands for, and what you offer customers. Focus means developing a brand that stands for something and says you are specialized in a particular area of work or goods. Consumers want a business focused on something, whether it's mobile brake repair, personal car accident repair litigation, or a real estate tax specialist, consumers want someone who knows their niche.

When you sell too many services or products, and your elevator pitch is a clear expression... And we're doing this... And that... And give those; it might take time to focus. Today, the market is competitive for just about any industry, and more so for the interest of a customer while selling the business. By specializing in something and doing it well, you maximize your airtime without as much effort and create popularity. Focus on your core skills and most profitable products or services—you will usually find it easier to get clients, and the company will be more competitive.

However, focus doesn't mean you need to do everything in the company yourself. When you are ready to expand, hire employees, assign tasks, and build a team, the emphasis is equally important to a business owner and essential to them. The emphasis is now shifting to how to handle and encourage the scale. It takes intense focus to recruit, train, and put people in power positions within the company.

The businessmen I've seen who don't reflect on this and just throw unnecessary tasks at their employees are often quickly in trouble. No one had said it was easy to build a company. If you take the path of entrepreneurship, it focuses on the one person who has the most in the business to gain or lose. Spend the time and resources to give the company the attention it needs to develop into a self-supporting organization; then, you can enjoy a successful business owner's returns.

IMPORTANCE OF FOCUS IN BUSINESS

Many managers and owners like to believe they are focused on a decent level of business. However, it's easy to get overwhelmed with the many problems and changes that your company faces on a daily basis.

It is worth staying the course, though, as there is a range of really powerful benefits to a strong business emphasis. Some of those are discussed below.

- Better marketing

The benefit of focus, first of all, is that it leads to better marketing. How? Because you can understand your worth better than ever before.

In today's technology world, where everything is available at the click of a button, businesses are facing a lot of pressure, and it can feel tough to keep up. The only real secret to success, however, is knowing the unique value proposition.

You can craft a superior product or service by concentrating on what you can sell that the competition can't. And consequently, these changes can be incorporated into "new and improved" marketing.

- Long Term Superior Planning

What's the opposite of good business focus? In short, it's reactive thought. There's a significant danger when we let ourselves be distracted by different changes and challenges. In fact, you'll spend too much time and money merely responding instead of doing something new and innovative.

You will create a long-term vision of success for your company better by having a strong business emphasis. This allows you to create a better strategy for long-term execution, which helps differentiate you from the competition.

- Good Customer Service

Customers are a key part of any company. That simple fact, however, is very easy for companies to forget!

Why? For what? Most companies end up losing out in the weeds of doing too much better and doing it too soon. Simple principles such as customer service can be left behind by concentrating on too many issues at once.

A strong focus on your market, however, means never losing your customers' sight. And you'll be able to develop customer-centric market ideas, above all else.

- Forward-Thinking

We discussed earlier how a strong outlook on business would help with long-term planning. In addition to developing potential growth plans, such an emphasis helps the business build the next big breakthrough.

Chances are that everyone in your market niche is trying to find the next big thing. And "search" is the keyword, because most companies don't want to invest time and work to innovate. You don't have to just hope with a strong business emphasis that you'll "find" something innovative; you and your team are going to go ahead and build something.

The Bottom Line: Now, you know the focus of business and what it can do. Can you help yourself get it started today?

FOCUS IN SPORT

Focus is an important part of sports success. Focus helps performers to listen to the signs in hand and to focus on the tasks to be successful. The ability to focus is crucial because it provides an opportunity for performers to achieve their objectives.

Focus is one of the most important instruments in the psychology of sports. Whatever sport you play in, the ability to focus is crucial to success. Does your mind ever wander when you're in the middle of a rehearsal or a competition? If so, the efficiency is taking on a hit, because the mission at hand is not entirely focused on you.

- Know what you need to concentrate on: the clearer you are about what you want to focus on, the more likely you are to remain focused on the factors that contribute to your success.

- Focus on what you can control: you have control over your own actions and attitudes— nothing else. Keep the focus in here. If you focus on results (things you have no control over), then you create unnecessary anxiety. Reflect on the method, and you increase the likelihood that there will be positive results.

- Stay relaxed under pressure: The focus decreases when you are nervous and anxious. Find ways to remain calm in moments of high pressure, such as taking deep breaths, stretching muscles to relax them, engaging in productive exercises to keep your attention where it needs to be, or listening to music that keeps you focused.

- Cue words: Cue words are simple words and sentences that remind you of your focal points. Repeating words and phrases like soothing, playing hard or fast feet can remind you to focus on what you need to do. If your mind is focused on words of your cue, then your body will obey.

- Develop effective routines: a funnel-like routine channels your focus and prepares you to compete. The rituals help you stay focused on the right things and avoid the entrance into your mind of many possible distractions. For example, listen to three or four songs on your mobile device or laptop before games to get ready, or eat a particular meal, arrive at the playground in sufficient time to get ready, or go through a specific type of warm-up.

- Using visual imaging: practice watching yourself do exactly as you wish, concentrating precisely as you want to concentrate. The more your mind trains in focusing on the right things, the more it will respond. Mental visualization is actually seeing yourself act as you wish well before you even step into the playing field. Imagery teaches you to see how you're going to perform, encourages you to think about what's most important in an excellent performance, and helps you to relax by focusing on things that are within your control and to an outstanding performance that matters.

- Rate your concentration daily: Keep a journal where you rate your focus level before and after every practice or competition. Clear, regular evaluations are crucial to your success. By being constantly mindful of enhancing and evaluating your focus, you will do so automatically. This kind of daily "internal muscle" work in practice and games will gradually improve your focus.

But what should athletes focus on?

This can be answered by describing various focal elements that lead us to types of focus in sport.

TYPES OF FOCUS IN SPORT

Focus can vary from narrow to wide.

- The broad focus is taking in a lot of information. Think of it as streetlights or lights at a field or arena—this light shines in a wide area and helps you to see a lot.

- A narrow focus is taking in little information. Think of this as a laser pointer—this is a very small thing, and you have to focus on something very important, so you can't see many things.

Also, the focus can vary from being external to being internal.

- Looking outside of yourself is an external focus.

- Inner or internal focus looks inside of you.

Such four areas combine to create four different focal forms.

A broad-external focus is assessing the situation.

- While trying to play a long pass, a soccer player may scan the field–noticing the movements of his teammates and the possessor when passing the ball, and the opponents.

- A tennis player will determine his or her opponent's position on the right without looking at him and then play to the left.

- A pole-vaulter can check the field of competition and detect weather conditions.

A narrow-external focus is focusing on 1 or 2 specific cues.

- A soccer player like Lionel Messi may look at the foot positioning of his opponent while trying to dribble him. That is how he does when he tries to dribble the likes of Sergio Ramos, Marcelo, James Milner, and so on.

- A distinct stare at a soccer ball while it bounces in order to control a given long pass perfectly.

- A pole-vaulter might choose to concentrate on her hip rotation.

A broad-external focus is used for research and preparation, including designing a game plan or strategy.

- A lacrosse player may formulate a plan based on what he sees and thinks can occur in the broad-or narrow-external context.

- A softball player will decide where she wants to hit the ball on the basis of what she sees in the wide-outside target. Also, she can think about what pitches the pitcher has thrown and made an educated guess about what pitch to expect next and how to change her technique when in the batter's box.

- A pole-vaulter can assess whether it needs to make any adjustments to the wind strength and direction of its vault.

A narrow-internal focus is employed to acquire mental training or control an emotional state.

- A soccer player may boost his confidence by reminding himself that he was successful in his last game. One, in particular, is Gabriel Jesús, a striker of Manchester City, against Everton. If there is a time you want to help this player boost his confidence, it is definitely against Everton. Just call on him as your striker.

- A football player may take a deep breath to manage his anxiety before taking a penalty shoot. One, in particular, is Cristiano Ronaldo, and he hardly misses a penalty shoot. He is a goal machine.

- A stage dancer may mentally rehearse her dance moves before going on stage. I had done this many times but not to dance. I had done this many times but not to dance.

Successful athletes know:

1. WHAT they should be focusing on and
2. WHEN they should be focusing on them.

FOCUS IN ACADEMICS

The focus can be the difference between accomplishment and failure. Without that skill, creeping in and sabotaging the most important goals in life is easier for problems.

Genuinely successful people strike a balance between their career and personal life.

Scattering your energy and attention between too many tasks will cause you to lose sight of original objectives. You're struggling to learn how you can plan to achieve them because you're unsure what they are. That's a significant contributor to failure.

Most successful people understand focusing on significance. You don't need to be super smart or a genius to outscore your competitors in school, company, or business, to be more successful at any cost. Everything you need is better and more efficient time management by reducing time-consuming practices.

Effectively using time because you can't create it. As a great leader, business tycoon, or scientist, everybody has the same 24 hours. What one does in the same 24-hour cycle differentiates a successful man from a failing one?

Focus on things that will help you move in the right direction.

People are taking focus for granted and paying the price to disregard it.

Think of anything that you do without focusing constantly. You may be successful in the process, while you are likely to fail in progress because you will not be able to understand or explain why one thing leads to another without a focus.

Consequently, the focus is a quality essential for finding, gathering, and analyzing the necessary information central to what we do.

All involved in our personal and professional lives distract us in some way or another.

1.   Discover distractions, and then do away with them.

Next, consider what distracts you from attention, and then attempt to popular the distracter. It's crucial to get organized and trained accordingly before you take on new tasks.

Now that you have identified your distractions by creating behaviors and lifestyles that hold those distracters away, you gradually need to remove these.

2.   Keeping Boundaries is necessary.

It is a must to be between people and interact with them. However, it is important to set boundaries between you and others if you need some time to complete your tasks by yourself.

You need to be in a position to set limitations for yourself on such tasks. That is all about discipline, after all. Discipline does not make life monotonous and dull despite the common belief but instead brings the right balance to your life.

Not just isolating yourself from other people and getting rid of things that annoy you, but also being confident while you're doing something important.

3.   Losing concentration can mean becoming irritated and impatient.

Anxiety starts building as the next step toward progress on the ladder may feel like a daunting task. And how do you alter that?

A lack of focus affects every aspect of your life. As a result, all your relationships will start to fail when you're more irritable and anxious. For you to reach your full potential, this vicious cycle has to be broken.

Focus means giving attention to what's important in your life. This focus will help you do a better job simply because we pay all our attention to it.

How to Remain Focused on Academics

Much distracts a student from academics, such as Smartphones, social media, television, Exhaustion, social pressure. The persistent, continuous stream of possible obstacles faced by students today is larger than in the past at any time. That doesn't mean that you can't do anything about it.

I'm going to show you the methods which work for me. I still consider myself a student because learning never stops as long as we live on.

1. CUT THE CORD — Drive off the grid.

I don't have to persuade you that technology presents a possible challenge for today's high school students. Any parent who reads this article undoubtedly knows how difficult it is to get a student to concentrate on doing something constructive with smartphones, social media, television, music, and video games all around us.

Indeed, even today, most academic research requires a particular type of technology.

Luckily there's a lot we can do about it. Any of the following measures will help you protect your students from the overwhelming effects of modern technology- maybe for as long as they can get some study done.

• Turn over the phone: Have you ever had your Smartphone seized maybe for a week or month? You will experience a great lot of leisure time which can be used to study. I once had a friend whose phone was seized for about three weeks. The way he answers questions in the class surprisingly changed, increased, and he gave another definition of himself. If you research and study further about this, you will discover that this will likely improve student's health and well-being, as well.

• Turn off the data connection: even the best-students frequently begin to work or research on a device and instead find themselves inexplicably idly surfing social media or the internet. The senseless, unintentional return to diversion is unlikely with your computer's data connection off.

• Get away from home: We all know that most of our devices live in our houses. They surround us as we try to work and research at home and call us out. If we work and study elsewhere instead, we can naturally decrease the number of technical distractions that we have available. You can go to the library; you can go out for a picnic, but you'll have books on this and so on instead of food.

2.	SLEEP, SLEEP, SLEEP— Live longer, be happier, be more knowledgeable.

Many studies show that having enough sleep actually makes us happier, smarter, and actually allows us to live longer. Also, the average high school student needs a little more than nine hours of sleep every night, and I'll suggest at least six hours for more senior school students.

You certainly have witnessed this in your own life; I know that I have. I am less successful, less satisfied, and less alert when I fail to get enough sleep. In comparison, my mood increases when I am vigilant in maintaining the time I spend sleeping, I feel happier, and my success on the job or learning is quantifiably better. Help your student sleep more, then. If you've had other ideas in the past about how much sleep your student should have, or how necessary it is, now set them aside without guilt or humiliation, and commit to secure your student's future sleep without hesitation and compromise.

3. GET UNCOMFORTABLE — And don't get back relaxed until you're done.

My mother used to tell me, "The days you find yourself unhappy are the days you get to know yourself more and more."

This approach to increase student concentration during research is highly successful and understated. Students may enhance their success greatly by carefully selecting their studying environment and committing to staying in that area until the research is complete.

For example, I'll always suggest to my students that they go to the library (leaving the phone somewhere else and shutting off the data connection) and commit to remaining in the library until they've finished everything they've been studying for that day.

I think the comparative boredom of sitting in a dark, dull library with no technology to encourage them also spurs students to be very successful–just so that they can finish off and get back to doing things they enjoy. This is the approach that works for me to perfection. I can't research at a place that has some distracting factor, noise. I love to research in a completely silent setting. When I was in high school, my parents ensure that no-one makes noise and distracts me while I want to study. I was well respected for taking some academic awards to my house.

If you don't think this technique works for you or isn't really necessary, try an experiment. Devote two hours to studying at home, and then spend two hours researching with all of your computers switched off in a library. Pay attention to how successful you are, and plan to be surprised in each setting.

4. SEE THE TARGET— Set simple, written goals and check progress.

Specifically, the act of sharing goals with a friend, such as letting your student share his or her goals with you, and then daily progress reviews with that friend, was established as a distinctive factor between the higher and lower success levels.

In a simpler sense: make your students write down and share their academic goals with you. Help keep your student accountable by reviewing his or her progress towards these targets regularly (for example, on a weekly or monthly basis). This technique will greatly increase the odds of the student attaining them.

Help your student get a clear perspective on his or her academic objectives. Help him or her take the time to think about it and consider its importance. And when your student completes them, help them take time to savor the achievement, and re-record it.

I could remember my chemistry teacher when I was in high school. He would ask me what I was up to every term. He would advise me on how to achieve my set goal for the term and keep an eye on my performance because I had a great rival in my class. It was really fun back in days like two political parties aspirants aspiring for the same presidency, with each one having his supporters.

Always remember this summary;

• Mental toughness- decision and zeal to go to school,

• Self-discipline- attendance in school,

• Focus- attentiveness in school. It is only when you are attentive in class that you can understand and gain the information or knowledge that is being passed to you.

Your ability to focus until you get the desired result justifies your mental toughness

EMOTIONS AND MENTAL TOUGHNESS

In the field of emotional intelligence mental toughness, or the capacity to be resilient and sensitive in difficult circumstances is seldom considered.

Nevertheless, good leaders recognize that being mentally tough is actually very reliant on emotional intelligence: you cannot be mentally tough and have low emotional intelligence.

In reality, not only do the best leaders understand the importance of emotional intelligence to mental toughness, they develop and optimize it. I know empathy is paramount. Because of their strong leadership skills, many leaders brought on board end up burning out and tired workers every day when they are harsh on their employees. It sounds like, and it might actually be bullying. Not everybody answers to a strong, no-nonsense, non-empathic dictator.

Emotions do not indicate that you are weak. In some cases, alpha-style leadership is successful, that is, military applications.

However, this sort of leadership does not translate well into the civilian world, where leaders need to understand the complexity of their workers at some point. Only ask them to do their job and that's not taking into consideration the various emotional, mental, physical, and other problems that workers may have. That doesn't require the leader to have feelings, not to mention. It sounds like bullying, and it could be, actually. Not everyone answers to a dominant, non-nonsensical, non-empathic dictator.

Emotions do not mean you're weak. Leadership in the alpha-style is effective in some situations, that is, military applications.

Nonetheless, this kind of leadership doesn't translate well into the civilian world, where at some stage leaders need to consider their employees' complexities. Only expect them to do their job and that doesn't take into account the different social, behavioral, physical, and other problems that employees may have. That doesn't include feelings for the chief, not to mention.

We can clearly see how emotional intelligence can help provide people in leadership positions with a supporting role, people with friends or relatives who are going through a difficult time, or just anyone for whom the more competitive, alpha-style is where they are relaxed.

<u>Relationship between mental toughness and emotional intelligence</u>

A frequently asked question is the relationship between mental toughness and emotional intelligence. It's a good question and it has a potentially complex answer, like all the best questions.

At its simplest Emotional Intelligence defines the degree to which you are sensitive to the individual emotions and feelings of others when you say or do something that somehow impacts them. It also explains how emotionally sensitive you are to other people's actions, words and deeds.

It's about the emotional response to the world around you, basically. As a result of that sensitivity, it doesn't necessarily indicate how you will react.

Mental toughness is a definition of something similar but significantly different. It is a personality trait that assesses attitude when dealing with stimuli such as stress, pressure, and difficulty (how we think and feel). Such factors may include an emotional response. Mental toughness is all about your responsiveness to those stimuli and how you are likely to respond by virtue of Mental Toughness' 4 components (the four Cs).

Nonetheless, it is difficult to easily summarize the possible difference and relation between Emotional Intelligence and Mental Toughness.

So someone with high Emotional Intelligence and high Mental Toughness may be sensitive to other people's emotions and feelings and will be successful in controlling their response. Research shows that someone with low emotional intelligence and high mental stress may be insensitive to other emotions and feelings, and in this case, their high mental toughness may manifest in apparently "thick-skinned." And so forth. Nevertheless, the same study also revealed that those who are more emotionally hard often appear to be "more comfortable in their own skin," which can often suggest that they are more open to communicating with others and their emotions and feelings. The idea is that Emotional Intelligence could even be a mental toughness type.

A link with the characteristics of these three Emotional Intelligence-Moods Management; Self-Motivation and Relationship Management can be seen.

The new thinking around Intelligent Emotions is perhaps more interesting. This resonates strongly with the scale of Emotional Regulation in Mental Toughness and indicates that individuals with this type of Intelligence are able to influence the mood of others around them through (authentic) displays of emotions and feelings. This in turn will give the person positive feedback and help them to control mood and emotions.

A perception being that Intelligent Emotions are better than Emotional Intelligence.

Difference between Mental Strength and Emotional Intelligence

The secret to your personal and professional success might be to grow both.

It's a big question because there are many assumptions about what it means to be mentally strong and theories about how emotional intelligence can be created.

The Definition of Emotional Intelligence

Over the years the definition of emotional intelligence has changed. It is the ability to understand how people feel and react, and uses this ability to make good decisions and to prevent or resolve issues.

Emotional intelligence in certain situations can give people a competitive advantage. A high emotional quotient will not automatically lead to higher academic performance— such factors are more dependent on Intelligent Quotient.

Emotional Quotient (EQ): or emotional quotient is characterized as the capacity of individuals to recognize, assess, regulate and express emotions.

Intelligence Quotient (IQ): is one of several standardized tests designed to measure the intelligence of a person.

Components of Emotional Intelligence

Five factors listed for Emotional Intelligence include:

1.	Self-consciousness- Self-consciousness is the ability to recognize and appreciate your feelings and drives and their effect on others.

2.	Internal motivation- A love for work that goes beyond money and status, like the inner dream of what's important in life or the pleasure of doing something.

3.	Self-regulation- Self-regulation is about redirecting destructive urges and moods, as well as being able to think before acting.

4.	Empathy- Empathy is the capacity to grasp other people's emotional nature and willingness to handle them according to their emotional reactions.

5. Social Skills- Social skills include the ability to manage relationships and to build relationships with others through finding common ground.

What is Mental Strength?

Mental strength and mental toughness are often used interchangeably. But there's a good chance they're not the same thing, depending on how someone defines mental toughness.

Mental toughness is often used when people refer to elite athletes or Navy Seals—and many measure their bodies to the extreme by seeing how much pain they can withstand.

Yet luckily, most of us don't have to race on a broken ankle or threaten our rivals physically. So that sort of resilience is not an ability that most of us need in daily life.

Being mentally strong doesn't mean acting harshly. It's about being aware of your feelings, learning from painful experiences, and living by your beliefs.

There are three main components of mental strength:

1. Regulating your thoughts- Regulating your thoughts involves learning how to usefully train your brain to think. That can mean ignoring self-doubt or replacing self-criticism with concern for oneself.

2. Managing your emotions- Being mindful of your emotions helps you to consider how your thought and actions affect certain feelings. It may include accepting emotions— even when they're uncomfortable— or it may mean behaving counter to your emotions when those feelings don't do you good.

3. Positive actions- Choosing to take action that will improve your life, even if you are struggling with motivation or delayed gratification, is crucial to becoming mentally strong.

THE MAJOR VARIANCE

Emotional intelligence is a part of the strength of thought. Yet mental strength goes beyond feelings and tackles the thoughts and behaviors that influence your life's overall quality.

Mental strength involves the creation of everyday habits which create mental muscle. It also entails giving up bad habits which hold you back.

The good news is that anyone can increase their emotional intelligence and develop strength of mind. And those skills will serve you personally and professionally well.

<u>Emotions and how do they relate to mental toughness?</u>

In the sense of Mental Toughness, the importance of this concept is that it resonates well with the sub-scales of Emotional Regulation in the model 4 Cs.

A simple way of explaining this is as follows: Imagine going to the theater to watch the well-known character performed by a great actor. The house is full of 500 people in the theatre.

Actors are trained not only to say the words but also to use body language, expressions, and so on to express their performance's full meaning. It means the audience understands not only what the character is saying but also understands why these words are being spoken by the character. That includes the feelings and emotions behind the words. This way, a good actor hits most, if not all, of the audience.

Actors are often prepared to "exaggerate" feelings and emotions to ensure that the viewer understands this full meaning.

Just imagine you're in the crowd now. Whose feelings and emotions are you reading from?

Mostly, you'll be reading the emotions and feelings of the character. Not those of the actor standing opposite you.

You may also be emotionally reacting to what you are getting.

So where is the "knowledge"–either in the transmitter (the actor) or the receiver (the audience).

A great actor is completely capable of playing a wide range of characters, some very different from their own personalities, convincingly.

What, in our everyday world, could this mean?

Most of us interact with other people, and when we do we impact people around us on mood and performance. Nonetheless, sometimes we put on a performance, particularly if we want to portray a happy and positive person when we actually feel depressed and potentially distressed. We don't want to reveal our true feelings, otherwise, the atmosphere and culture of our surroundings could be badly affected.

We use our emotional control in these cases to set aside what we think and feel and to show people a more optimistic set of emotions and feelings. This has to be genuine in that you are presenting a set of emotions and thoughts you would normally display if you were really happy with it. Anything else would have probably not worked.

The goal should be to retain or even raise the mood around you that will feedback to you positively, and help improve your mood and emotions about what has happened. That is a type of modification of cognitive bias.

Then the idea here is that emotionally hard people learn how to handle adversity and loss, but also understand how to maintain a positive attitude and a positive outlook. That is, they should control their emotional response in such a way that it affects the emotions and feelings of those around them, and where it is helpful, it also helps to lift their own emotions and feelings and to stay positive in the face of adversity.

This is consistent with our understanding of how the scale of emotional control could work in the four Cs model. It does not mean insensitivity to a mentally tough adult. We can control their feelings, clearly.

Finally, there's no implication here that people should never express their real emotions and feelings. That's more about time and location. There are clear advantages of expressing what you really feel–but perhaps to those who can be trusted in dealing with this, and who may be able to understand and help you. There will be times and places where you have a responsibility to maintain calm, and it will be more fitting to control and cover your emotions. This is particularly true if you are a leader and your moods or feelings-positive or negative-can have a significant impact on those around you.

It's a field that will be further explored as it has the potential to be relevant and important for a large number of people.

How to be mentally tough without sacrificing emotional intelligence

You might believe being mentally strong means ignoring your emotions. In reality, it is the reverse.

Mental toughness— the ability to be flexible and concentrated, to make decisions and work even in the midst of challenging circumstances or adversity — is a prized quality among leaders. Yet mentally tough, effective leaders aren't those who ignore their own feelings or those of others. In other words, the most mentally tough people typically should have the highest quotient of emotional intelligence.

In 2018, a research found that mental toughness is "based on the ability to use emotions effectively." It also found that mental toughness levels were positively associated with higher emotional intelligence, which it described as "the capacity of a person to direct his or her thoughts and actions based on a reflection on the feelings and emotions of themselves and others."

You do have interesting insight into their own and other emotions. Three things psychologically challenging leaders know about the feelings here:

1.   EMOTIONS ARE NOT A SIGN OF WEAKNESS

When companies become less hierarchical and flatter in their management structures it is important to consider other people's opinions and emotions. Taking unilateral decisions without knowing how they will affect others— and the resulting emotions — no longer works. Leadership styles must be successful in adjusting to the organizational culture.

But it's also important not to allow your emotions in high-stakes circumstances to be used against you.

Athletes may get into the state of the zone which may seem emotionless but is in fact highly attuned to what they feel and what is happening around them. Lionel Messi would keep his emotions under wrap and control since the opponent would always try to get him to respond in some way during a game situation. He would always monitor the aspect of his emotional state, and then let it out once the game is over off the pitch or in the dressing room.

2. EMPATHY IS ESSENTIAL

While I was the General Secretary of my department, I saw many fellow students struggle with some specific area of their academics, especially Physics-related courses. Even though I was so busy, I still created time out of no time to tutor them about what they don't understand in Physics. Even when I felt extremely tired, I did struggle to take the tutorials. They could see the tiredness in my eyes and many times they will tell me "Sorry" and even get me lunch packages. This empathy made me more responsible in their eyes and I became more mentally tough. My father always says to me "the way you handle little things is the way you will handle big and great things".

If you think you are mentally tough and have no empathy, you are only swimming in the middle of the ocean. Mentally tough people have empathy because they live for the benefit of others. Their lives are not theirs and they cannot be selfish enough to contemplate on giving up because they love people behind them, not the benefits in front of them. Please let us appreciate our parents for that. My father would say that he is financially stable enough to change his car every year but he can't because of his children's well-being. That is empathy! Please let us appreciate our parents. Mentally tough people really care for others' well-being.

3.   FEELINGS IS NOT IMMERSED IN THEM

You can be good at understanding feelings without letting them overtake you or preventing you from making the best choices. Often people get stuck in empathy— feeling what the other person feels, particularly when those feelings are intense. Many people get the ability to put themselves in the shoe of another.

At times, we also need to use perspective-taking, which is a more rational view of the emotion without actually feeling it and relying on compassion, which means supporting the person feeling the emotion, even without inherently doing the same. It's easier to make straightforward, rational choices when we can distance ourselves from strong feelings.

True mental toughness is the ability to feel and understand and to be empathetic about what people feel. But also, to be able to have the control for where that doesn't make you overcompensate, in one way, where those emotions pull you into a vortex or the other way, you can't allow any feelings.

WAYS INTELLIGENT PEOPLE DEAL WITH IMPOSTOR SYNDROME

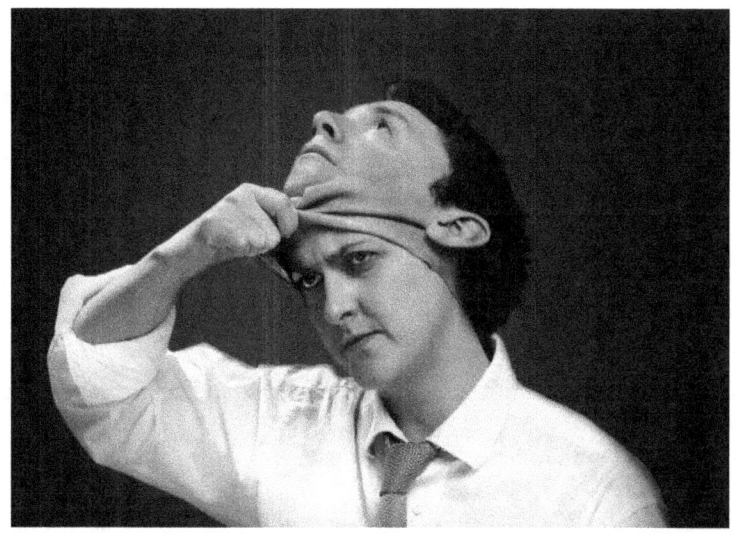

First, what is the condition of the Impostor?

Impostor syndrome (also known as impostor condition, impostorism, fraud syndrome, or the perception of impostor) is a psychological trend in which one questions one's successes and has a constant internalized fear of being revealed as "fraud." Many witnessing this trend remain convinced, given external evidence of their competence, that they are frauds, and do not merit all they have accomplished. Individuals with impostorism attribute their success to chance incorrectly or view it as a result of deceiving others into thinking they are smarter than they consider themselves to be. Although early research focused on the prevalence of high-achieving women, impostor syndrome was recognized as having an equal effect on both men and women.

Types of Impostor Syndrome

This psychological condition represents a perception that given evidence that indicates you are qualified and quite effective; you are an inept and incompetent failure.

In short, harmfulness is a hot mess. It can also take different shapes, depending on the context, temperament, and circumstances of an individual. If you are familiar with the feeling of waiting to "figure you out" for those around you, it may be helpful to consider what sort of impostor you are so you can solve problems accordingly.

1. The Perfectionist

Perfectionism and imposter syndrome often go hand in hand with each other. Think about it: Perfectionists set themselves excessively high expectations, and when they fail to reach a target, they experience serious self-doubt and worry about measuring up. If they know it or not, this group can also be freaks of nature, thinking they have to do it themselves if they want something done right.

Not sure if that is accurate for you? Ask yourself:

- Did you ever be accused of being a micromanager?

- Do you have big problems delegating? Would you feel frustrated and disappointed about the outcomes even when you are able to do so?

- Would you accuse yourself of "not being cut out" for your work and ruminate over it for days when you miss the (insanely high) mark on something?

- Do you know your job has to be 100% perfect, 100% perfect?

Success is seldom satisfactory for this sort since they feel they could have done even better. But that is neither good nor successful. Owning and enjoying successes is necessary if burnout is to be avoided, contentment found, and self-confidence established.

Learn to take your errors in phase, and see them as a normal part of the process. However, force yourself before you're ready to act. Push yourself to start the project which you have planned for months. Truth is, the "perfect time" never occurs and the job will never be 100 percent flawless. The earlier you can recognize that, the happier you'll be.

2.   The Superman/woman.

Because people who experience this phenomenon are persuaded that they are phonies among colleagues in real-deal, they also force themselves to work harder and harder to calculate. But for their insecurities, this is just a false cover-up, and job stress can affect not only their own mental health but also their relationships with others.

Not sure if that is accurate for you? Ask yourself:

- Should you remain at the office later than the rest of your staff, well past the point where you've done the necessary work that day?

- Do you get stressed when you are not working and feel that downtime is totally wasted?

- Have you lost your interests and ambitions, dedicated yourself to work?

- Do you feel like you've not really earned your title (despite numerous degrees and achievements), and you feel forced to work harder and longer to prove your worth than those around you?

In reality, imposter workaholics are addicted to the affirmation which comes from working, not the work itself. Start training yourself to isolate yourself from outside validation. No one should have more control than you to make you feel good about yourself— even your supervisor when they give the approval stamp for your idea. On the flip side, learn to take seriously, not negative, constructive criticism.

As you become more attuned to internal affirmation and are able to cultivate your inner confidence that states that you are professional and knowledgeable, you will be able to ease off the gas when you gauge how much work is fair.

3. The Natural Genius

Young says people with this form of talent feel they need to be a natural "genius." As such, they measure ease and speed based on their ability as opposed to their efforts. To put it another way, if they take a long time to learn something, they would feel shame.

Such types of imposters, including perfectionists, set their internal standards incredibly high. But the styles of natural talent not only judge themselves on the basis of ridiculous expectations, they also judge themselves on the basis of getting things right at the first attempt. If they can't do something easily or fluently, they sound their alarm.

Not sure if that is accurate for you? Ask yourself:

- Used to excel without a lot of effort?

- Have you got a track record of "straight A's" or "gold stars" in everything you do?

- As a kid, have you often been told that you were the "smart one" in your family or peer group?

- Would you dislike having a mentor, because you're able to handle things yourself?

- Does your morale crumble when you face a loss, so failure to perform well creates a feeling of shame?

- Do you often avoid challenges because doing something you're not great at is so uncomfortable?

Try to look at yourself as a work in progress, to move past this. Carrying out great things requires lifelong learning and building skills— for everybody, even the most optimistic individuals. Instead of punishing yourself when you don't meet your impossibly high standards, identify specific, changeable habits you can improve over time. For instance, if you want to have more effect at the workplace, working on enhancing your presentation skills is much more effective than swearing off speaking at meetings as "just not good at."

4. The Soloist

Sufferers who sound as if they were asking for help are what Young calls Soloists. Feeling independent is OK, but not to the point you deny help so you can prove your worth.

Not sure if that is accurate for you? Ask yourself these questions:

- Do you believe strongly that you need to do stuff yourself?

- "I don't need anybody's help." Sounds like you?

• Should you view demands in terms of project specifications, rather than as a person's needs?

5. The experts assess their knowledge on the basis of "what" and "how much" they know, or can do. Believing they're never going to learn enough, they risk being seen as inexperienced or ignorant.

• Unless you meet every single educational requirement, do you shy away from applying to job postings?

• Are you continuously looking out for training or certifications because you think you need to elevate your skills in order to succeed?

• Can you relate to feeling like you still don't know "enough" even if you have been in your role for some period?

• Do you shiver when a person says you are an expert?

It's true there is always more to be known. Striving to enlarge your skill set will definitely fuel your professional progress work hard and keep you competitive on the job market. Yet pushed too far, the desire to search endlessly for more information may in fact be a form of procrastination.

Begin the process of learning just in time. This means learning ability when you need it– if your roles change, for example– rather than hosting information for (false) comfort. Realize when you need it there's no shame in asking for help. Tell a coworker if you don't know how to do something. If you can't figure out how to solve a problem, tell a supportive supervisor for advice, or even a career coaching. Mentoring junior colleagues or volunteering can be a perfect way to discover your inner expert. If you share what you know that not only rewards others but also helps you heal your dishonest feelings. No matter the specific profile, if you struggle with trust, you're far from alone.

If you've done it at any point in your career, you've chalked up your successes to opportunity, charisma, relationships, or some other external factor at one time or another. What is that unjust and unkind? Take the opportunity today to start accepting your strengths and welcoming them.

Emotional intelligence can help you more quickly shake off impostor syndrome. Okay, here's how.

The impostor syndrome phenomenon is simply the illusion that' I can't keep going.' Which isn't true, right? Therefore, the cognitive illusion is thinking,' To this long-term goal, I cannot hang in there. I really won't do it. I can't keep up.' And it does happen to the contrary even in the face of substantial evidence.

One hundred percent of senior-level people said they "never" get impostor syndrome in their self-talk and behavior showed signs of that. Of those who said they didn't know what it was, 75 percent showed clear signs of it, with the percentage for those in senior roles spiking to 100 percent.

Yet emotionally smart people have a different set of skills that help them to better handle impostor syndrome than most. We understand that there is an opportunity for them to replace, let's say some sort of reactive or emotional response with one that is more logical, rather than just going with gut reactions or their first reaction.

People are more able to overcome cognitive distortions because they are able to identify and control their feelings. Here are five aspects that people with impostor syndrome are emotionally intelligent:

- PAUSE AND REFLECT

If people who are emotionally smart feel insecure or uncomfortable they are often able to take a beat and assess the situation. They understand that both the sensitive portion of our brain, the amygdala and our more logical center of thought, the neocortex, are focused on our reactions.

Whoever is emotionally smart will pause when the amygdala triggers an emotionally based reaction and has an internal dialogue. We agree that something you think of something you feel is not always the objective truth. It is just a variation of how the brain responds to something initially. And often they can relax that reaction and think about the situation was more rational before a conclusion was made.

SEEK PERSPECTIVE

While you're in the grip of impostor syndrome, seeking confidence can seem like a challenge— especially when you're the highly accomplished person whom everyone else goes to for guidance and pep talk. Turning the tables can be tough, and asking for help.

Even people who are emotionally smart will let themselves be vulnerable to getting the help they need. He says having a trusted friend, partner, or counselor who can help you express what you feel and discuss is an important step in leaving behind those feelings. This perpetuates the impostor syndrome when you're not telling anyone about it.

- BUILD A CASE

Emotionally intelligent people are seeking evidence from the world around them, so they can determine facts that either support their emotional reactions or disprove them. So, to get a sense of whether what they hear is a misunderstanding or not, they look at their own achievements, preparation, and track records. In some cases, a stretch assignment, or a new, more difficult job, spurred the impostor syndrome. Reviewing the behaviors and experiences that contributed to that opportunity will give you a sense of whether or not what you experience is real-life-based.

- GIVE THEMSELVES A BREAK

Emotionally intelligent people realize that there are 7.7 billion people on the planet, and each of us is born with a sense of inadequacy, vulnerability, uncertainty, anxiety, and fear.' People who are capable of controlling their emotions realize that feeling a little behind everyone else is part of the human condition and not an incapacity to act. Instead, they keep on showing up and doing the things that scare them.

When you show up inside, when you feel about yourself, that's the way you are handled by the universe. When you step into your own skills and confidence, even if you're nervous, you're going to get better than when you're responding in fear or trying to falsify your way through powerful emotions.

- ACKNOWLEDGE GOOD INSTEAD OF WAITING FOR PERFECT

People ought to be continuous learners in an information economy. It's easy to feel left behind as technology, patterns, and workplace issues shift on a dime.

Emotionally intelligent people are more likely to have an attitude of growth which helps them to acknowledge that they are not going to be good at all. Those who become trapped in the notion of being thought leaders and need to "know it all" are more vulnerable to impostor syndrome because they have trouble admitting what they don't know.

As an alternative, people who are emotionally intelligent welcome curiosity for finding out what they do not know. If you are curious and keen to extend your knowledge base in another direction, that may give you a different perspective from another group of disciplines. That will improve your performance in your current role.

A common illness is the impostor syndrome. Developing your emotional intelligence skills— so much sought-after by many organizations — can help you overcome that when it happens.

How to work with someone who isn't emotionally intelligent

You'll understand the difficulties if you've ever interacted with someone who's unpredictable, temperamental, moody, or just grumpy. Here's how to cope.

Over the past 20 years, few psychological characteristics have been praised more than emotional intelligence (EQ). Loosely defined, it's the ability to control your own emotions, and to read and manipulate the emotions of other people.

When recruiting and improving employees and managers, companies attach increasing importance to Emotional Quotient. Unfortunately, many managers have a low Emotional Quotient, which for their workers is a common cause of anxiety and stress. If you've ever worked for someone that's unpredictable, temperamental, moody, or just grumpy, you'll understand the difficulty of putting up with a low boss of Emotional Quotient. Even if organizations and their managers make progress in the growth of the Emotional Quotient, you will always have to learn how to deal with low Emotional Quotient people, including sometimes a supervisor. No amount of coaching will change someone with problems of chronic anger management, serious deficiencies of empathy, and lack of social skills.

Selecting more leaders based on their Emotional Quotient will improve the overall standard of our leadership— and increase the percentage of women in leadership. But as that is unlikely to happen soon, it is important that you learn to adapt to lower Emotional Quotient people, particularly when they are responsible with you. Here are four guidelines, based on science.

CONCLUSION

Thank you for reading all this book!

While this book is now drawing to a close, the path to inner peace is just starting. I'm sure you'll feel more happiness and tranquility in your life as you slowly begin to incorporate some of the ideas into this novel. Don't think you're not alone. In every world, there are millions of highly sensitive individuals trying to cope with a weak nervous system, too. You will truly enjoy being a highly sensitive individual now that you have the coping skills to survive in our overstimulating environment.

There seems never to have been a time in human history when more than a handful of odd men and women became equal partners. Men and women now seeking equality are doing something different, and had a better understanding of the overwhelming essence of their mission. Recent research suggests that our first responses to a human are instinctively focused on the biases we experienced as infants, no matter how unkind or unwelcome such prejudices now seem to us. This is actually some very old conditioning by humans to support us defend our in-group by devaluing any outgroups. But now it certainly causes trouble, in every corner of the world. This study also shows that the only real difference between racial, patriarchal and non-conscious individuals is the conscious effort taken by the latter to overcome their implicit biases acquired in childhood.

However, a lack of discrimination doesn't mean sameness in all matters.

Instead, it implies that control is fairly divided according to the desires and capacities of each individual. HSPs will lead to the development of this kind of gender equality because we are excellent at recognizing our internal systems, even our biases, and can understand that class, like personality, requires a different-but equal mindset on the part of everyone. We are also exceptional at understanding the implications of all possible strategies, so we can see that an imbalance in dominance between the sexes will never contribute to the trust and intimacy that we are trying to build in ties. Gulf of hatred, then all we hated in ourselves was hurled/projected at them so that our hand thought all nice and theirs all evil.

You have already taken a step towards your improvement.

Best wishes!

www.ingramcontent.com/pod-product-compliance
Lightning Source LLC
Chambersburg PA
CBHW070938080526
44589CB00013B/1560